When Seagull Found His True Self

WRITTEN AND ILLUSTRATED

BY WENDY KEMP

DEDICATION

This book is dedicated to humankind.
May we all find true happiness.

Hi I'm Sid, Sid Seagull. I live on a balcony behind a square art deco clock, in the middle of the facade of a hotel, in the seaside town of Eastbourne. I have the most magnificent view of the pier and the sea from my balcony. I have lived here all my life, with my mother and four little sisters. When my sisters were very young and couldn't fly, the diamond shaped iron railings, which run along the balcony, saved them from the perils of falling from such a height.

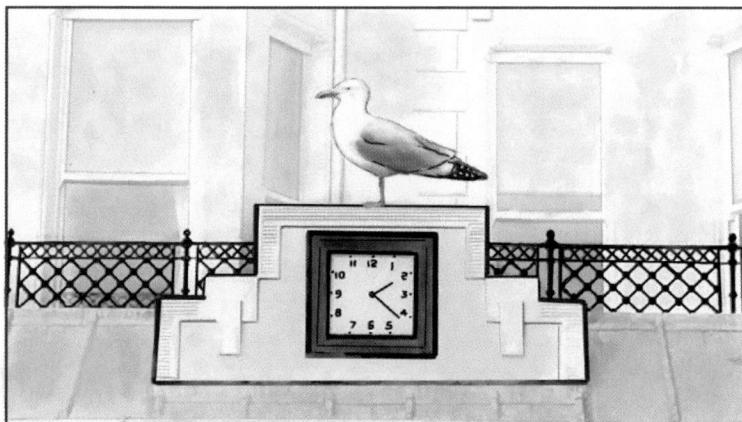

You may think that I am incredibly lucky to wake up each day with such a wonderful view of the sea and being able to breathe in the fresh salty air, but no. Every morning, when my sisters were young, I was woken up by the noise of those screeching and squawking, bickering and brawling, tremendously annoying little sisters. It drove me crazy watching their demands on my poor mother. I could even hear them from the old part of town, which is miles away. One day the noise was so unbearable I bought a woolly hat to cover my ears. Everyone nicknamed me Hatty.

My mother worked nights at the local fish and chip shop on the road opposite the pier. When the shop closed for the evening, she came home with tiny bits of leftover fish to feed me and my sisters. That kept them quiet for a few minutes!

When I was old enough to be on my own, I was able to escape the noise at home and fly off. I once met a very wise Owl called Eckhart. He told me that there are three ways to deal with a challenging situation:

Number 1- change the thing that is driving you mad;

Number 2 - accept the thing which is challenging you;

Number 3 – remove yourself away from the situation.

Well, I couldn't change my sisters' behaviour and I couldn't accept it, so I removed myself from them. I spent most of the time searching for food on the promenade near the pier. I didn't work so I couldn't pay for my food and I was too lazy to go out to sea to catch fish. I wandered around eating all the chips that people had dropped from their greasy white paper bags. It didn't take me long to work out that you can find more chips next to the benches than anywhere else. The benches near the pier with a good view of the sea were the prime spots for dropped chips.

One crisp winter's morning the cloudless sky was a powder blue and the sea was flat like a mirror. The sunlight shimmered on the surface of the sea like a beam of glittering sparkles. I stood still, transfixed by the beauty that was before me. The incredible view pulled my eyes from scanning the pavement for food. My mind went blank for a while; it was as if I had lost myself in a magical moment.

A little starling was sitting beside me. Surprised, I woke from my trance, not knowing how she got there. Her eyes were closed; she looked so calm and peaceful. She opened one eye and turned to me. Softly, she whispered, 'When you realise you're not a drop in the ocean but the ocean experiencing a drop, you will realise who you really are.' And off she flew.

I had no idea what that meant and started walking.

You are not a drop in the ocean,

you are the entire ocean in a drop. - Rumi

It didn't take me long to realise that it was on sunny days that I found more chips. On rainy days, humans would retreat to their cars and munch away while peering out of steamed up windows.

As the years went on, more and more seagulls came, eventually getting to the point when the number of seagulls outnumbered the chips. I got more and more frustrated. I often thought, 'Hey, this is my patch; I was here first'.

I didn't have many friends. Then one murky grey day when I hopped under a bench, to my surprise there was a pigeon and half a crispy chip. 'You have it,' she said smiling, 'I've had one already'. This kindness took me aback as kindness wasn't something I was used to. 'What's your name?' she asked. 'Sid,' I replied, a little bit wary as no one ever spoke to me. 'What yours?' I asked at the same time as picking up the chip.

'Hattie' she chirped. I instantly took a liking to her as she had the same name as my nickname. Little did I know that this was to be the start of a lifelong friendship.

Hattie was a homing pigeon. She wasn't really a fan of chips; she liked cake. Actually, 'liked' is a bit of an understatement; she ADORED cake. Often, we would hang around the benches near the sweet-smelling doughnut shop for hours. We'd wait for tiny crumbs and specks of sugar that had fallen from the humans' mouths as they devoured their sticky, sugary doughnuts. It wasn't long before I liked cake too.

My favourite cake was a blueberry muffin. They were incredibly crumbly and the blueberries smelt like a sweet perfume. Hattie's favourite was a French strawberry tart made from neat, overlapping layers of strawberries on top of crème pâtissière in a sweet pastry base and covered with a light sweet glaze. Strawberry tart crumbs were very hard to find, but 'oh my' when you found them, they tasted like heaven. Hattie once told me her dream job would be to work in a French patisserie. In this dream job, she would be able to eat as many delicious cakes as she wanted to all day long. She explained wistfully that every week she would work her way along the different rows of pretty cakes, tasting all the sugary, gooey, heavenly delights.

Most evenings, Hattie and I would walk together and tell each other about our problems. I would tell her how hearing my sisters bickering and squawking all the time made me so annoyed. She would also open up to me about her problems. She hated the fact that she loved sugar so much and hated it when people told her to go on a diet or to fly more. 'It's not that easy!' she would say tearfully. She felt very self-conscious and thought other pigeons were always judging her. We hugged. I feel it is very important to have a friend to talk to about your problems - and to listen to theirs.

Every evening, be it rain, hail, or shine we would sit together under the pier, until it was so late that I knew my sisters would be asleep. While sitting under the cold and damp pier we shared stories of the day about all the stupid humans and stupid birds we had encountered. Our minds were always full of chatter about the stupid seagulls.

We often saw the same little starling that spoke to me about the ocean. She always sat at the same place on the beach next to the pier. 'Can you see that starling?' I whispered to Hattie one day. 'She sits so still with her eyes shut for ages before flying away.' 'That's Suzi,' Hattie whispered, 'she told me once that she is practising meditating. She's a student of Zen Master Kingfisher and has found her true self. She sits here every day before sunset, quiet and motionless. She said she connects to the Divine Source, then flies off!'

I didn't really understand what Hattie meant but Suzi looked so peaceful and calm. I wondered how that would feel.

Our conversation was interrupted by squawking and shrieking from somewhere up on the road. We flew to the top of a street light to get a better view of what was happening. A huge fight had broken out outside the chip shop where my mother worked. There was a mass of seagulls fighting. It had been raining all day so chips had been scarce; now it looked as though a human had dropped a whole portion of chips all over the pavement. I had never seen such a kerfuffle and such despicable behaviour.

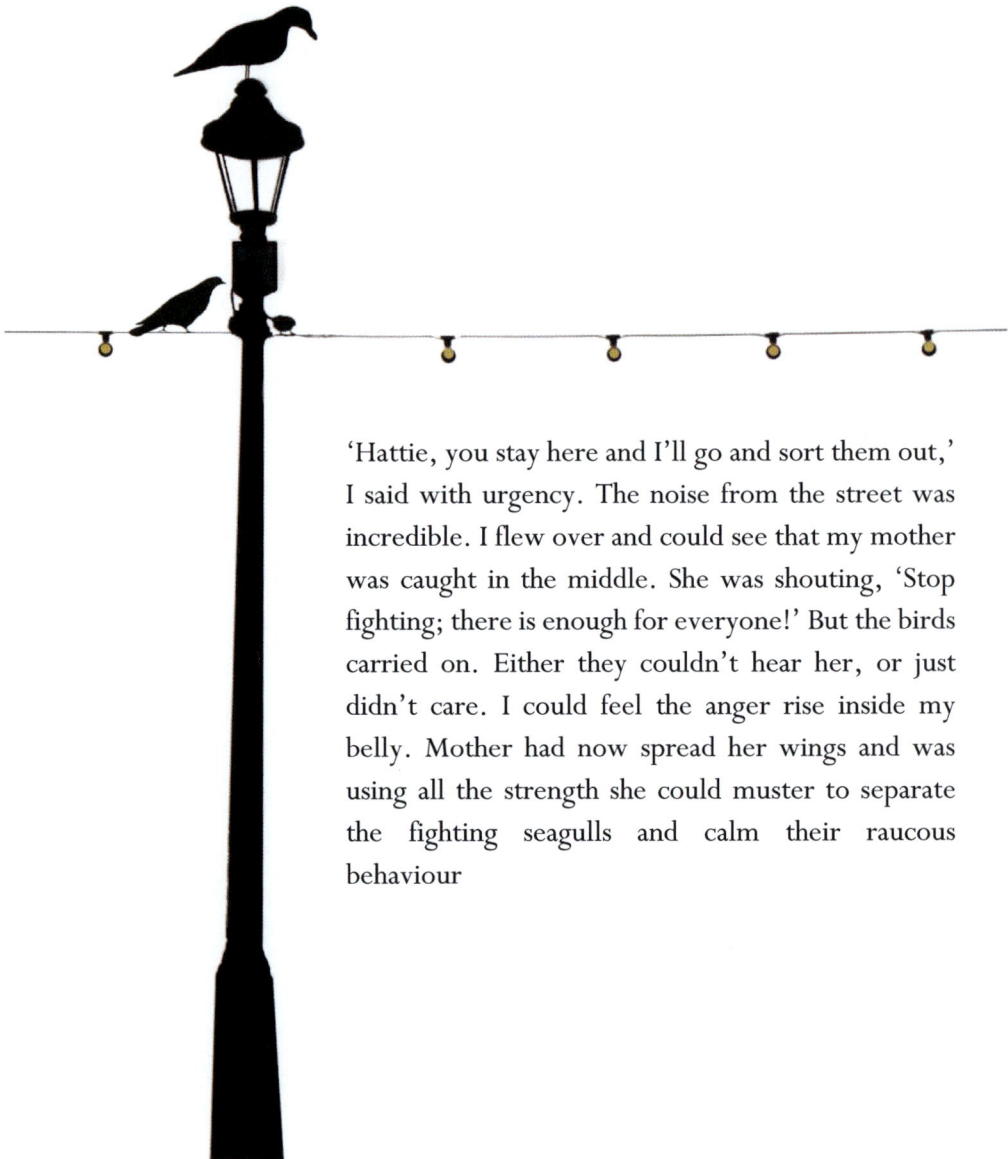

'Hattie, you stay here and I'll go and sort them out,' I said with urgency. The noise from the street was incredible. I flew over and could see that my mother was caught in the middle. She was shouting, 'Stop fighting; there is enough for everyone!' But the birds carried on. Either they couldn't hear her, or just didn't care. I could feel the anger rise inside my belly. Mother had now spread her wings and was using all the strength she could muster to separate the fighting seagulls and calm their raucous behaviour

As I got closer, I saw one of the gulls had knocked her to the ground. She looked to be in pain: they had damaged her wing! I had never felt so much anger. 'Where are the Crow Police now?' I thought bitterly. I felt disgusted that not one single bird had stopped fighting to help my mother. With difficulty, she made her way from the middle of the boisterous ruck. I spotted a fishing net which was part of the decorations above the fish and chip shop. Quickly, without much thought, I grabbed it with my beak and hauled it over the fighting gulls. Trapped in the scruffy net, they immediately stopped fighting as their wings and feet were tangled in the twine.

I didn't want any more to do with these birds. I checked my mother's fragile wing as carefully as I could. It wasn't broken but it was bleeding. I walked her home and bandaged her wounds, still feeling furious about the events of the evening.

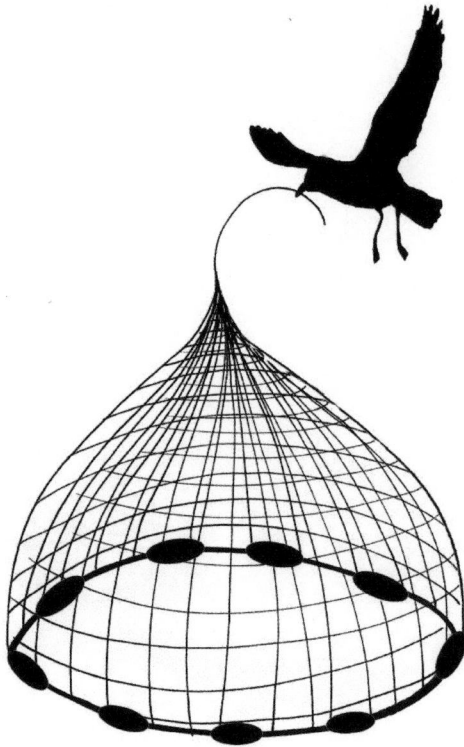

The next morning, I woke up in such a rage. All I could think about was the selfish and disorderly behaviour of the seagulls. Over and over again I pictured the fight and I was becoming more and more angry. No wonder seagulls have such a bad reputation with people.

Then something happened which changed my life forever.

One night I decided not to go home. I flew around town still searching for the seagull which had knocked over my mother. I was tired from lack of sleep and I was still very angry. I spent all night searching but didn't find him.

Next day at about a quarter to twelve, the first humans started to line up at the fish and chip shop waiting for it to open. At twelve o'clock on the dot, the door opened, and it wasn't long before the smell of vinegar filled the air. I went to sit on top of a nearby chimney pot, watching the humans eagerly opening up their white packages of fish and chips. I watched as they blew on the first few chips before putting them in their hungry mouths. I watched with my beady eyes, like a hawk watching over a mouse, waiting for the perfect moment to swoop down and catch my prey. I didn't care about the consequences of my actions: I was tired; I was hungry; most of all I was still furious.

As the last chip was heading for its destiny, I had to intervene. I swooped down at full speed, a hawk with my target set. I turned my head slightly on my approach to get the correct angle. I snatched the chip from the greedy human's hand just as he had opened his mouth to eat this last chip. With a flick of my head, I tossed the chip in the air; beak wide open I gobbled it up in one mouthful.

Unbeknown to me, there, perched on the bandstand on the opposite side of the street sat a police crow. He had watched my every move.

Sergeant Crow read me my rights and cuffed my wings together. 'This is absolutely bonkers!' I said furiously. 'I only stole one chip. Where were you last night? How is this fair? How is this just?' Sergeant Crow didn't listen; he marched me down to the police station.

My anger festered and grew as I waited in a police cell. I had to go to court and when I was given six months in prison, I became even more irritated and started shouting at the judge. That was a big mistake. The consequence of my shouting at the judge added four years to my sentence. Unbelievable! I knew there was no point in arguing again – I might be given a life sentence.

Back home, I had developed a reputation for being angry and there was a rumour around town that jail would make my anger even worse. This was actually far from the truth. In fact, jail was the best thing that could have happened to me. Ironically, it was jail which set me free. I learned how to let go of the anger and hatred in my mind, how to let go of stress, jealousy and envy and I even found space in my mind to think of others, not only myself. I was able to see that I had been a prisoner in my mind with all its negative thoughts which filled my head all day and night. I found a place of stillness, a place of calm, and a place of joy. I found a place inside me that had boundless love for myself and for others. I became aware of another part of myself: there was something more to Sid, something beautiful which can be found in all living things. This was what Hattie meant when she said Suzi had realised her 'true self'. I became aware that there is something far greater than who we think we are. This something is so hard to explain in words, but it is a nature, an essence which feels calm and peaceful and still. This essence of our being is the true nature of ourselves. I had woken up to realise that there is something more to Sid Seagull than all of Sid's past and personality, opinions and physical form. There is a spiritual aspect on a deep level in all of us.

Let me explain how this happened.

Jail was incredibly boring. It was damp and had the smell of rancid fish. We had nothing to do all day and we weren't allowed out to fly. Every bird had its individual cage and a very scary Raven guard watched over everyone, making sure there was no 'funny business'. Rumour around the cages was that Ronny Raven used to work at the Tower of London and you know what happened to prisoners there!

On my left was Morris Magpie. He was put in jail for stealing some fabulously expensive jewellery from a museum in York, which was once a house belonging to a very rich Peacock. He had planned his theft for months but it all went wrong when the Crow police caught him on CCTV.

As I looked to my right, I saw cages of all kinds of birds. All the birds inside looked as if they were sleeping: so still, so calm, so peaceful. I followed the line of cages. Right at the end I saw a bird who was also very still. This bird, however, was not in jail. He had the most beautiful azure blue feathers that stood out so brightly against our dull, locked cages.

The bird directly next to me opened her eyes and looked at me. 'Hi,' she said softly, 'I am Shreya Starling'. I asked what she and the bullfinch and goldfinch next to her were doing. 'We are all meditating,' she replied. 'We have all learned how to quieten our minds and connect with Divine Source. Zen Master Kingfisher is teaching us how to find Enlightenment.'

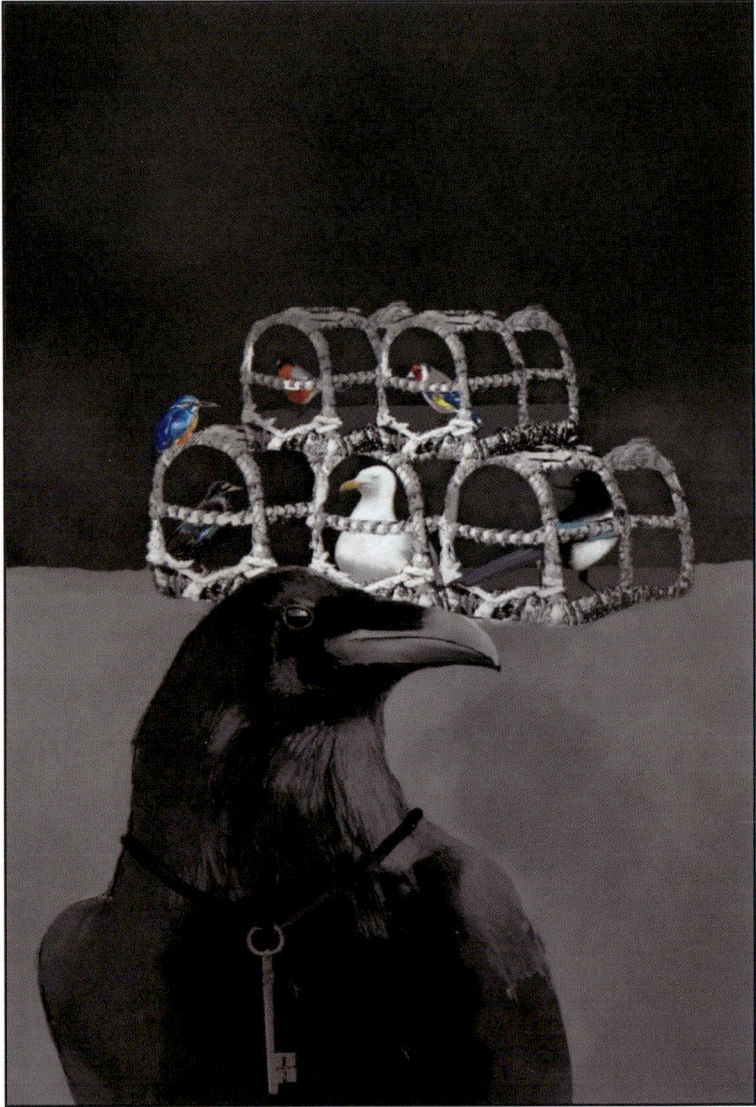

I remembered Suzi Starling mentioning something about this. Shreya continued to explain that through meditation practice as well as mindfulness we can all connect to our true essence which is also known as the Divine Source, God, Buddha Nature, Universal Spirit, Consciousness or whatever you want to call it; as essentially, it's the same thing.

I looked a bit bewildered so Shreya carried on. 'We are like layers of an onion,' she tried to explain. 'We can learn to see our different layers such as "that's my personality layer, that's my mind layer, that's my emotional layer, that's my attributes layer and that's my history layer." All these layers are part of our form. When we have peeled away all of these layers, which are part of our form, we find something still and something pure. When we find this place, it feels as if we're sitting in a boundless energy of love. This is the divine essence found and connected with all living things. It's like a glowing light deep inside you. When you have found this place, you also begin to see things from a new perspective. You begin to want to connect with it more, and the more you connect with it the more it grows and glows. You notice nature's beauty more and you start to see that there is good in everyone, but sometimes it is hidden underneath the layers. We realise that there is more to us than we once thought. This is called "self-realisation". When we wake up to our true selves, it's called an "awakening".'

'Wow that's incredible.' I said, kind of understanding what she meant, but not knowing what it would feel like. 'So basically, inside all of us is a pure interconnecting place of love?' I asked timidly, scratching my head, trying to grasp this exciting information I was being given.

Shreya nodded, she told me that it's impossible to explain it properly as it is far beyond what our bird brains can understand. It is far beyond words. It is more of a deep knowing.

I sat down for a moment trying to take it all in. I thought how wonderful it would be to be rid of all my anger, stress and negative thoughts. I looked over at Zen Master Kingfisher. 'And what is Enlightenment?' I questioned. Shreya softly explained that Enlightenment is when you have infinite wisdom and feel that you are connected to everything and everything is connected to you. It is when you realise that you are not separate but are one with everything. Your thoughts about who you think you are (the form layers) are just the small aspect of yourself because your true self is so much bigger. You realise that you ARE the Divine Source having a bird (or human) experience.

When we reach Enlightenment, we come from a place of peace and love, we are able to trust in some great divine plan far beyond our understanding. When we let go of our ego thoughts and surrender ourselves to this nature, it is called 'being in the flow' and life seems to flow so much easier. We can even accept life's difficulties with grace and peace.

I scratched my head. She knew I didn't get it. I thought I would just stick to learning to meditate as a start and then in time, if I practised meditation and did things from the heart rather than from my mind, then I might find the divine essence in me. I liked the thought of feeling peace, joy and love all the time. 'This is just what I need,' I said to Shreya excitedly. Shreya continued, 'Zen Master Kingfisher taught Burt Bullfinch how to meditate, then Burt taught Gary Goldfinch the teachings and then Gary taught me. This is a special lineage. Because of my meditation practice, I am always calm and I never get stressed or worried. I am not frightened of change and I understand that there is a reason for most things that happen in our lives. If everyone in the world meditated there would be no fear, anger or hatred and the world would be full of love, compassion and kindness.'

Shreya spoke with such love. I felt so peaceful just listening to her and even when she was silent it was as if she had a beautiful light around her which was full of kindness. I asked if she could teach me. 'Of course,' she said with a beaming smile, 'you're next in the line.' And so, the lineage went on. Zen Master's teaching of connecting to the Divine through stillness and meditation rippled its way to me.

I realised that before I was put in jail, I had been trapped in my thoughts all my life. I was constantly thinking about what I needed, consistently worried about my mother and constantly angry with my sisters. I was always thinking of how hard life was and how other birds didn't understand how hard my life was and how every other bird's life looked so much better and easier than mine.

I wanted to feel like Burt, Gary and Shreya. It was time to quieten my thoughts. It was time to still my mind and to find the peace and love that resides deep down in me which is connected to everyone else.

Shreya was great at teaching meditation. She had so much patience with me. I guess she had no choice as we were both stuck in jail and going nowhere. She said I must sit in silence every single day for ten minutes and in time gradually build it up to at least twenty minutes. At first, she said, I may not see or feel any difference but I must be disciplined every single day. I had to concentrate on my breath. I had to be aware of my breath going in and out through my beak. 'Well, that sounds easy,' I thought.

After three weeks of focusing on my breath for twenty minutes a day, I didn't feel any different. It was so much more difficult than I thought it would be. All I could think about was how uncomfortable the floor was without a cushion. After six weeks, I still felt no different. All I could think about was how Burt's breathing was so noisy during his meditation practice. After week eight, I had tiny moments of stillness but then my mind went back to thinking about my family at home and how my back ached. Week nine. Three deep breaths. In and Out, In and Out, In and Out…

I wonder how Hattie is…

There goes my mind thinking again! It was so much harder than it looked. Every time I asked Shreya how long it would be before I could think of nothing, she would add on even more months. It actually got to the point where I just gave up asking her and thought it will happen when it happens.

One morning while eating the six peanuts we were given for breakfast. I had a pressing question for Shreya which I had pondered about for months.

'Why are you in jail, Shreya? You seem the kind of bird that would do nothing wrong'.

'Well,' she said, chasing the last peanut around the plate before finally catching it, 'two years ago I went to India on the yearly migration to get away from the cold UK Winter. When I was there, I discovered that when I ate Burberry seeds my body felt so much better and I could fly better without getting so tired. I had never heard of them before so I thought I would carry some back with me for my long flight home. I didn't know they were listed as an illegal import to the UK. I was arrested at customs for having four Burberry seeds under my wing that I hadn't used on the journey. I was put in jail and here I am'.

'Wow' I thought in disbelief, 'I didn't know you could be arrested for carrying seeds.' I wondered if Barnaby Blue Tit knew this fact as he had gone to Ukraine to bring back a whole suitcase full of sunflower seeds.

As the weeks passed, my meditation practice became easier. There were days which went well and days when my mind kept butting in. As time went by, the butting in days became less frequent and I became less and less annoyed by them. Apparently, Burt had taken ten years to reach the same place of stillness that Shreya had reached in seven weeks. I desperately hoped it wasn't going to take me ten years. But I admired Burt: he was very disciplined and patient and he had achieved his goal eventually.

While in jail, I also learned the importance of mindfulness. When Ronny Raven gave me peanuts, I learned to be mindful when eating them. I tasted each one individually, noticing how it felt in my beak. I was starting to get better at noticing and being aware of every single moment. My silly thoughts and negative opinions and beliefs started to melt away. I was becoming more and more peaceful in my mind and I felt calmer as every day went by.

Four years went by and I never missed one single day of meditation and mindfulness practice. I felt so calm and peaceful that I wished all the birds and human beings in the world could feel like this. I looked over to Morris, who looked sad. I knew he was worried about his family. I decided to teach him everything I knew in the hope he would find this realisation and feel as I did.

It was an odd feeling the day that Ronny opened my cage to set me free. Ironically, I felt grateful for being sent to jail. If it hadn't been for that challenging point in my life, I would not have met Shreya and I would not be the kind, compassionate, honest bird I am today. I would not have found that place within me which has boundless love and compassion.

As I said my goodbyes to Shreya and Morris, Shreya told me there would be more challenges to face in my life, as life is full of challenges. But if I carried on with the meditation and mindfulness practice, I would be able to cope with these challenges much more easily. I thanked her for everything she had done and turning to Morris I encouraged him to carry on with his practice.

Finally, I plucked up courage and I left to breathe in the salty air, see my mother and sisters and catch up with Hattie.

I found things had changed when I arrived home. My sisters were, of course, older and had stopped bickering. They helped Mum at the chip shop and had more responsibilities, which made them kinder and easier to live with. Mum was able to work a little less, so she wasn't so stressed, which meant our home had a calmer energy around it.

I spent more time just sitting on the beach. I did my meditation practice by closing my eyes and just listening to all the various sounds. I noticed the salty air more and I noticed more of the tiny things that I had once ignored such as the perfect spirals inside shells. I collected them thinking how pretty they would be if I made them into necklaces for my sisters.

For hours, I watched the waves roll onto the shore and listened to the whooshing noise of the tiny pebbles as they moved up and down the beach. All this wonderful nature had been there all the time and I had never properly noticed it. I felt a big warmth in my heart as if I was part of everything and I could feel this beauty internally. It gave me so much joy.

Suzi Starling said once that noticing the beauty in everyday little things and feeling so much joy was a way of connecting to the Divine Source that is in us all. 'Yes!' I whispered to myself, 'I can feel it now.' My chattering mind had gone and I felt perfectly happy with such a profound love. I was free from my thoughts and my personality. 'Had I found enlightenment?' I wondered. I wanted to hold onto that experience forever. I had so much joy, so much calm and peace and trust. I feared nothing. I felt like a lighthouse, beaming an amazing light all around me. I felt I was part of something so much bigger. I was Love; I was the Divine Source and I was here on this planet having a bird experience.

'I get it now,' I said to myself with such amazement and excitement, 'I get what Suzi said that day about not being a drop in the ocean
but being the ocean experiencing being a drop!'

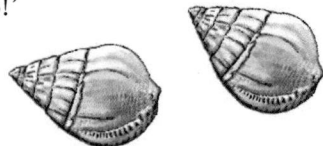

I caught up with Hattie and told her all about how to find her true nature. I wanted Hattie to feel as I did. It turned out that Hattie had had quite an adventure too in the last four years. While I was in jail, she had actually flown to France to train to be a pastry chef. She is currently working in a delightful patisserie in town called 'The Sweet Retreat'. She doesn't eat cake crumbs from under the benches anymore but treats herself to one very expensive cake every week. She eats it mindfully and savours every bite. She no longer worries about others' perceptions of her. She has made her dream come true. I was so pleased to see Hattie so happy.

The summer flowers in the gardens this year seemed to look brighter than previous years. I watched the bees going from flower to flower collecting pollen on their furry legs. One hot day I looked up over the neat row of purple lavender and saw a flash of blue at Poppy's Tea Room. It was Zen Master Kingfisher having tea outside.

I flew across to the café and went to see him. He smiled and nodded at the chair opposite, gesturing for me to sit down. There was another cup at the table. He knew I was going to join him. 'You have come a long way,' he said in his calm and gentle voice. I looked over at the gardens. It must have only been fifteen metres. Then I realised he meant I had come a long way on my spiritual journey. 'Yes,' I said, 'I feel that I now see the whole world from a different perspective. I want to say thank you for all that you have done and for all your teachings. I have found my true self. You have changed my life.' 'I'm proud of you,' he said, 'for being so disciplined and never giving up on your meditation practice.'

'Once you have attained Enlightenment, does it stay forever?' I asked eagerly. He replied wisely, 'Enlightenment is not a destination where you stay, rather it is a series of one moment of enlightenment after another.'

He dropped a grain of sugar in his tea and we both watched how the ripples on the surface got bigger and bigger all the way till they reached the edge of the cup. 'I see you understand Karma and how your actions, your words and your thoughts have an effect on yourself and others.' Karma was a new word to me but I knew he meant "the ripple effect". 'Yes, I really do,' I replied. 'Just the other day, I saw how my thoughts had an effect. I was watching an old pigeon with a poorly foot, he had a stick and was limping around over there at the bottom of that litter bin in the park.' Pointing with my wing to the overflowing bin, I continued, 'I felt sorry for the old pigeon and decided to send him a thought of kindness, compassion and hope that his foot would heal. As I sent the thought, immediately the old pigeon stood still and looked up at me. He took off his cap and gave one nod of his head before gently putting his cap back on and carrying on his way. That was the moment I had proof that our thoughts and prayers matter and that we are all part of something far greater than anything we could possibly describe. I knew then that we are all connected to each other like invisible interweaving cobwebs on some higher existence.'

Kingfisher closed his eyes while he took another sip of his raspberry herbal tea. After savouring his fruit tea, he got up; he smiled and nodded at me and left. It felt as if he had left a trail of light behind him.

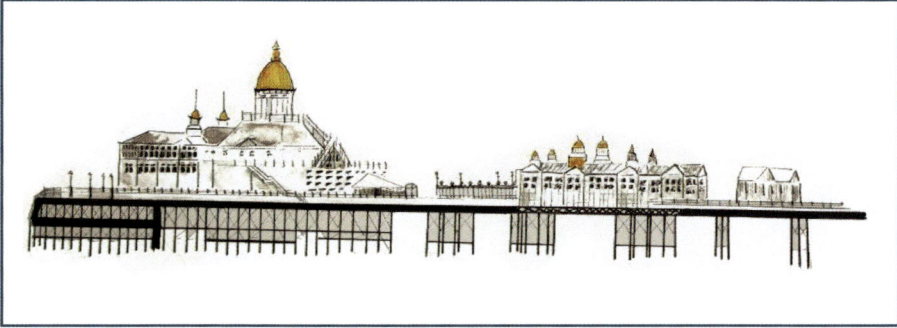

I walked slowly to the pier and decided that instead of sitting under the pier as I used to do with Hattie, I would sit to the side of it on the beach. Suzi flew down and sat beside me. I told her all about my time in jail, my awakening and how I now understood the profound meaning of being an 'ocean experiencing being a drop'.

Suzi asked me to join her on the wire to meditate together. I looked up and saw hundreds of starlings just like Suzi all sitting on the wire like tiny notes on a music stave. I thought it might be too tricky for me to meditate on the wire so I sat on a street light next to Suzi.

We meditated together just as the sun was starting to set. Sitting silently with our eyes open, we focused on the sea.

Our minds were empty and we sat in the stillness of the moment.

There was such a rich sense of peace and gratitude. After about twenty minutes I suddenly had a moment of inspiration. I had a lightbulb moment and turned to Suzi to tell her. But it was too late: Suzi shook her feathers and flew off, just as she always did after meditating. All the other starlings flew off too. Suzi turned her head to me and said softly, 'You have let go of your mind and have returned to your heart.'

I watched her as she flew into the centre of what seemed like ten thousand starlings. These small birds now appeared like magical notes, silhouetted against the orange sunset. I watched in awe and with such love; it pervaded my entire being. Mesmerized, I watched as they instinctively danced in perfect union around the orange sky. I could see how they were all connected on a divine level and how they moved as one. I had never seen a murmuration before; it was the most beautiful thing I had ever experienced. It was pure magic, pure love. And again, in the stillness of the moment, my thoughts melted away. I could hear their music and I was dancing too.

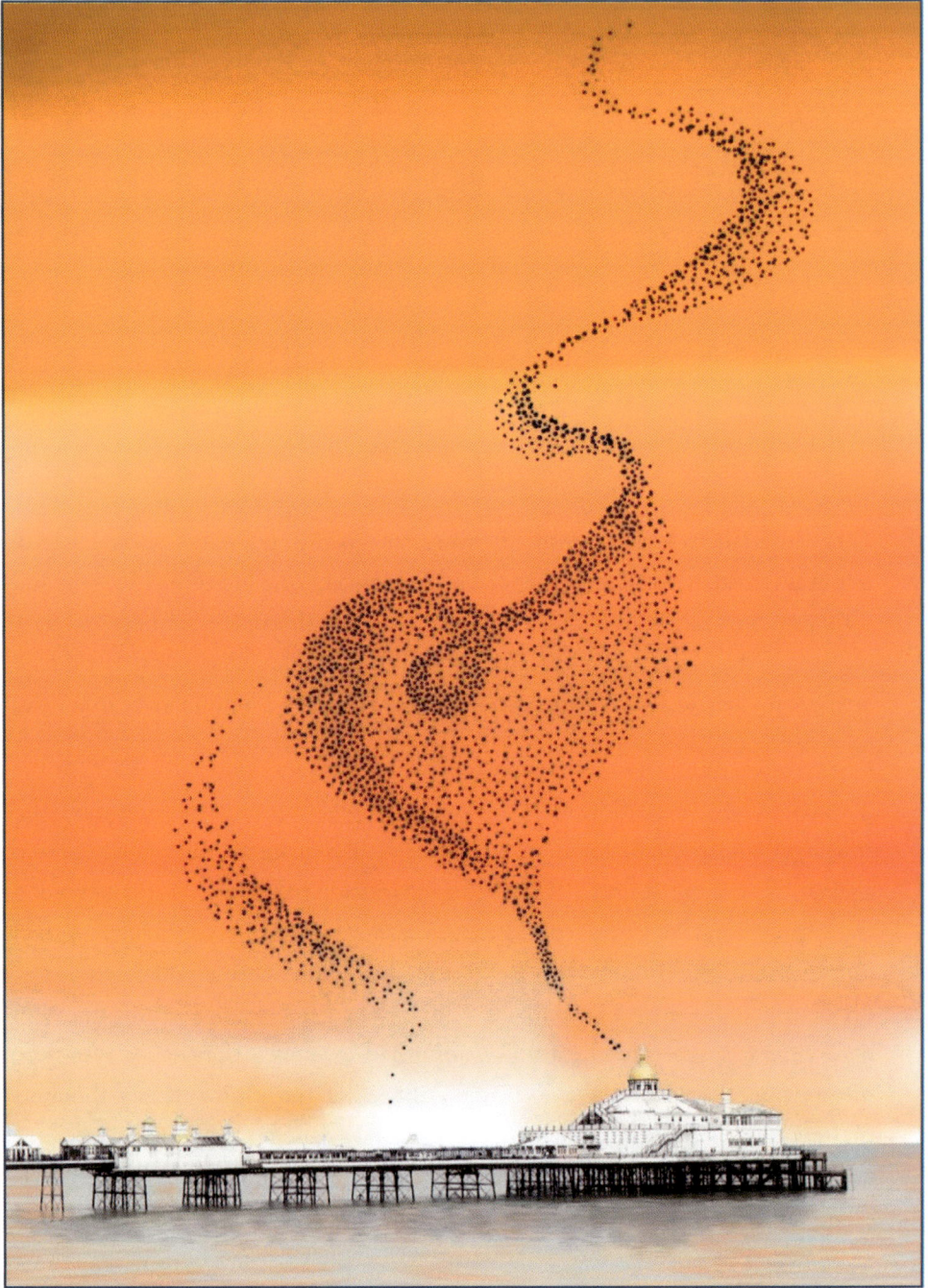

THE END

If you are wondering what Sid's moment of inspiration was then here it is:

Sid's lightbulb moment

Imagine you are a lightbulb.

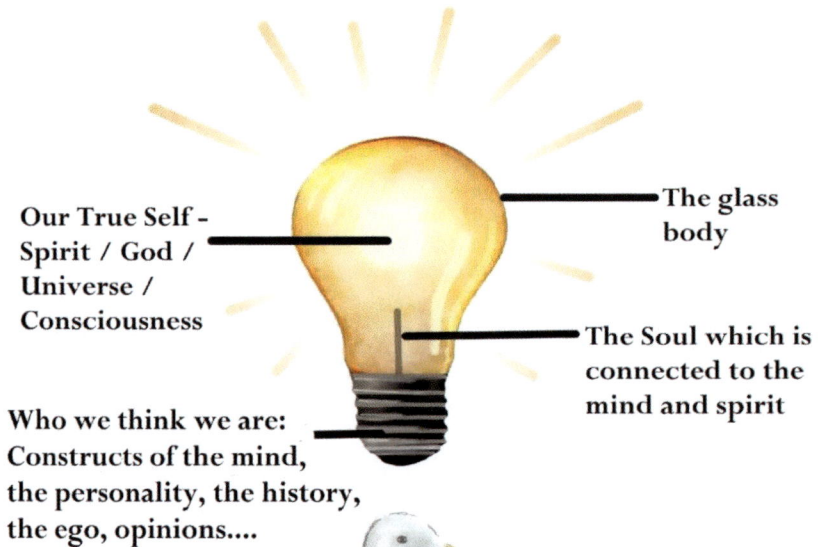

Our True Self –
Spirit / God /
Universe /
Consciousness

The glass
body

The Soul which is
connected to the
mind and spirit

Who we think we are:
Constructs of the mind,
the personality, the history,
the ego, opinions....

Other books written and illustrated By Wendy Kemp

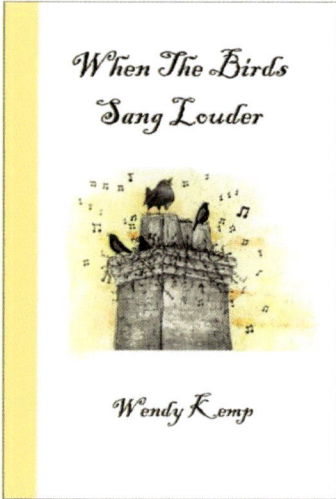

'When The Birds Sang Louder'
Blackbird tells his story about
the covid pandemic from his
wise perspective.

'Blue Tit's Visit To Ukraine'
Barnaby Blue Tit tells his story
about love, loss, compassion
and kindness.

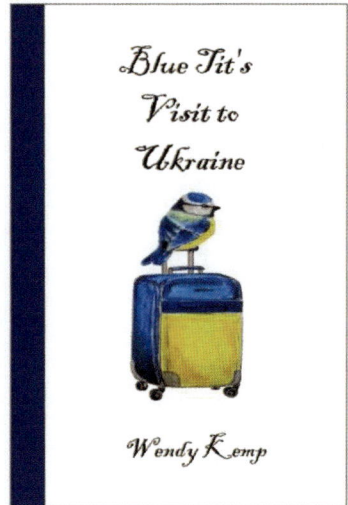

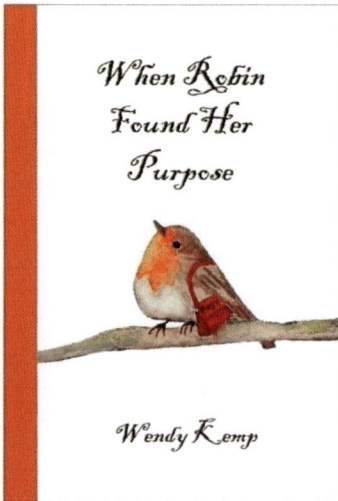

'When Robin Found Her Purpose'
Rosie Robin discovers her purpose
in life after her short visit to
the afterlife.

ALL BOOKS ARE
AVAILABLE TO PURCHASE
FROM AMAZON

Printed in Dunstable, United Kingdom

63818698R00022